*i*S◉LATION

'Throughout this collection unsettling daily experiences are made less disconcerting by the language of poetry.'

— Willem van Toorn
– Dutch poet, novelist, critic, translator

'These are poems from "A desperate world locked indoors, online,/Looking at heaven-blue screens for a sign", or "An hour's walk along this deserted beach,/Where hope advances in each wave's retreat"; they are poems steeped in longing for what was, and what may still be possible. Tom Petsinis' *isolation* gives us plangent moments of tense, witty, poetic remembering, with linguistic dexterity and a wanderer's desire.'

— Lyn McCredden
– poet and professor, Deakin University

Other works by Tom Petsinis

Fiction

Raising the Shadow

The French Mathematician

The Twelfth Dialogue

The Death of Pan

Quaternia

Fitzroy Raw

Poetry

The Blossom Vendor

Offerings: Sonnets from Mount Athos

Inheritance

Naming the Number

Four Quarters

My Father's Tools

Breadth for a Dying Word

Steles

Plays

The Drought

The Picnic

Elena and the Nightingale

Salonika Bound

Hypatia's Circle

Euler's Vision

iS⬤LATION

Tom Petsinis

ARCADIA

© Tom Petsinis 2021

First published 2021 by Arcadia
the general books' imprint of
Australian Scholarly Publishing Pty Ltd

7 Lt Lothian St Nth, North Melbourne, Vic 3051
Tel: 03 9329 6963 / Fax: 03 9329 5452
enquiry@scholarly.info / www.scholarly.info

ISBN 978-1-922669-94-9

Cover design: Alexia Petsinis, Wayne Saunders

Contents

Three Clouds

Almost at the travel zone's limit,
I'm driving to buy a masonry bit,
To drill and brace with steel rods
Exposed footings rigid with past
To a future pour carefully boxed,
When traffic lights stop me dead
For three white clouds passing by,
Preceding tonight's thunderstorm:
The first a faceless surgical mask,
An unreachable toilet roll's next,
Followed by the blue-bowed wig
Mozart wore noting his Requiem.
A green arrow prods me hard left,
Turning thoughts to concrete again.

Collective Nouns

A prohibition on gatherings of more than two,
I'm walking on a drizzling Sunday afternoon,
Isolated, weatherproofed, coat zipped to chin,
Through quiet Westerfolds Park dissolving in
Mist as it must've when a herd of dairy cows
Grazed here at ease, ruminating, unshadowed.
Rounding the manor house bricked on the hill,
I'm surprised by a mob of kangaroos, the still
Big grey upright, taut, somewhat apart, there
With the lookout's measured, defensive glare.
A flock of cockatoos invigorates a dead gum,
Sharpening black beaks, chattering in unison.
Further on, six crows sound a murderous tune,
Brooding, coronial, over my hooded solitude.

Toilet Roll Addressing Face Tissue

You've been in the limelight too long:
Keeping lips proper in public displays,
Complementing black at state funerals,
Stopping noses running amok with flu –
But with things turned arse over head
I'm now the celebrity everyone craves,
Crowds brawling desperately over me,
Raising high what yesterday they hid
Under a mountain of bright groceries.
Dear sister in white, we're really alike
Serving the body in moments of need,
But I won't be coy starring in my role:
I'll open closets secured from within,
Uncovering ends your glamour shuns.

Goal Posts

An afternoon mild with mid-autumn light,
On the footy ground a season postponed,
Ghostly lines clinging to thickening grass.
Completing the last lap of my daily walk,
I'm struck by the goalposts stranded there,
Estranged from what they've always been,
Not the pair that defined a six-fold space,
A contested opening to earthly paradise,
But, stripped bare of their protective pads,
Each suddenly separate, isolated in white,
Bereft of purpose a safe ten paces apart,
Shadows lengthening, skewed to the left.
I stand between them with tumbling heart
Both forefingers defying their pointless fist.

The Curve

1

With life more abnormal each day
And confidence lower than in war,
The curve's now on everyone's lips.
As fear skews the population right
The average person knows the shape
Crossed in red on the nightly news:
If it's steep, like the unscaled peak
That leads to a shortness of breath,
The virus may well crowd hospitals
But likely recede in several weeks –
If flatter, like childhood's green hill
Climbed unaware of legs and lungs,
We may escape with a collective sigh,
Based on a diminishing sample size.

2

The politics of age, gender, social class
Prescribe how different curves are seen.
Consider the one protruding like a horn –
For some it's crude capitalism at work,
Patriarchal, excessive, erect with pride,
The moment before its potency is spent.
The one having a more generous range
Is for others the promise of better times –
The gentle swell of the pregnant womb,
The loose breast rising round with milk,
Maternal comfort in this season of fear.
And for the few there's the shapely bell
That tolls in silence the growing count –
Its symmetry even death must observe.

3

Time's the only variable independent of life,
Continuous, proceeding with horizontal ease
From today's zero to tomorrow's arrowhead.
The positive count (the negative aren't seen)
Depends on how long it's been since the start.
When spikes shoot high on consecutive days
Logarithms show the human scale at a glance:
Small numbers shouldered powerfully by ten
Keep the axis from ranging through the roof.
Tomorrow we'll bow to this graph for a sign:
The curvature no longer breathtakingly steep,
Becoming less of a climb, until flattening off
To an hour's walk along this deserted beach,
Where hope advances in each wave's retreat.

Mathematics

In this muted time of death and disease
Maths has never been so intensely alive.
The daily count in Italy, England, Spain
Runs riot down Chile's elongated spine,
While Australia learns to hold its breath
And keeps it masked for several months.
A concept many still find hard to grasp,
Rate of change is almost commonplace:
Not as a limit, though, x nearing nought,
But the globe edging closer to the abyss.
Maybe more than words and metaphors,
Numbers hold the natural hope we seek:
The loved ones lost to ascending peaks
Are less than those left grounded in love.

Wars

When invaders came in my parents' time
Their weapons whistled over the village
Like a shepherd gathering flocks of souls –
People found shelter in each other's fear
And solace through closeness and touch
In cellars where old darkness was stored,
Mines thick with ghosts coal left behind.
Today's invader comes unseen, unheard,
Not in a cranial helmet but spiked crown,
Shutting us in our cluttered living rooms,
Distant from neighbours, family, friends,
With smartphones, laptops, iPads at hand,
Our words of comfort muffled by masks,
Lacking the mouth's incubating warmth.

Birds

Planes grounded, silent in their size,
Birds are now reclaiming the skies,
Opening distances with their wings,
Sound from the quiet around things.
Secateurs for beaks, crests up, loud,
Cockatoos tear oaks turning brown
For acorns wearing a monastic cap.
A magpie sipping at a dripping tap
Raises its heads, puffs out its breast,
And arpeggios on a soulful clarinet.
A bellbird's sharp, distinctive ping
Is the old Milk Bar's door opening.
As dusk hurries walkers in the park
Kookaburras take turns laughing last.

Patient Zero

As the New Year releases the Rat,
The woman of Wuhan lies in bed,
Congested, feverish, out of breath,
Her questions scattering like bats.
How and where did all this begin?
Fish gasping mutely in wet hands?
Restless creatures caged on stands –
Pigeons, pigs, endemic pangolins?
Or in what Granny would observe?
Bake an offering to the dear dead
When winter crowns the moon red.
Is this perhaps what she deserves?
Or is she Nature's stepping-stone
As it progresses from zero to one?

The Crest

Dad, how much higher to the crest,
How much further before we rest?
A little longer and we'll get there –
Count each step, not the empty air,
Those with heads in fluffy clouds
Stumble and fall on stony ground.
Dad, when we've left this behind
What's in store on the other side?
A steep descent that tests us more
By going backwards on all fours?
Or rolling hills in downward ease,
A path untrodden to unfished seas?
Climb, my boy, save your breath
For tomorrow's mountainous debt.

Conspiracy Theory

Conspiracies abound in troubled times –
Granny's is more grounded than the rest.
Of course the Earth's behind it, she sighs:
Our long-neglected mother is distressed
At how her prized garden's been spoiled.
Yes, she has feelings, a mind of her own –
Consciousness isn't from a god unknown
But like a creeper from sunlight and soil.
A lesson in how to protect and preserve,
She set a spiky crown on a crimson shell
As the belated Christmas gift we deserve.
Look, smiles Granny in her show and tell,
The smog's lifted, the wren's come back,
The daisy has opened the concrete's crack.

Viral Past

And now another virus springs to mind:
A kid at Fitzroy North Primary School,
I'm still mixing three languages as one,
Thinking, milk in hand, polio is Greek,
And afraid the double O would multiply.
Crew-cut Bruno's in the crowded yard –
A Cowboy chasing Indians with a limp,
Shooting straight with his fingered gun.
The click of that brace securing his leg
And stirruped under his thick-soled shoe
Has followed me more than sixty years –
And here I am, captive to a silent mask
Thwarting each breath, unable to outrun
This threat and hide in the shelter shed.

Catholic Good Friday

Taking out rubbish to the backyard bin,
I'm surprised by a glow from my right,
Through the cedar's shaggy silhouette –
The moon, masked by a thinning cloud,
Appearing all at once brighter and full.
Working remotely for almost a month,
Days reshaped to fit the laptop's screen,
(Even Friday has lost its heavenly feel)
I reflect: the autumn equinox has been
And Easter passed with an empty hand.
With the city bracing for a ring of steel,
(Homes like prisons, graves for some)
And darkness pushing deeper into day,
The moon glows in gold and silver foil.

Orthodox Good Friday

With numbers sounding the storm,
The white church is empty tonight –
We're caught in a crown of thorns
And a saviour's nowhere in sight.
The Crucifixion's an online affair:
Censer bells jingle the old hymns,
Puffs of fragrant smoke fill the air
Which viewers can only imagine.
A son is watching, drinking alone,
As *zoi entapho** contracts the nave,
Heart having surrendered to stone
When his mother opened the grave.
As for the Resurrection we expect –
Is it in the lab or the crimson egg?

---

*   *zoi entapho* – Greek: 'life is entombed', congregational hymn
   sung on Good Friday.

Angry iGen

No, she thinks, while scratching the crown
Tattooed on the inside of her arm's dystopia,
I won't be manipulated and sacrificed to fear,
Allowing my future to come crashing down.
Why masks, social distancing and cafés shut
For what's in fact nothing more than the flu,
Which, at worst, will pass in a week or two?
And then what of the budget's huge deficit?
I can read between the lines on their tongues:
It's really about the old protecting their kind –
Those Premiers, Presidents, past their prime,
No consideration for the rights of the young.
Yes, they'll secure their decade from death
While saddling idealists to a lifetime of debt.

Greetings

Suddenly bare hands are suspect,
As much as one's captive breath –
No telling where they have been:
Doors, coins, a glossy magazine
That changed a shopper's mind.
I meet a neighbour on the street
Who's not walked in some time –
I nod and without thinking reach
Out for his hand rising for mine,
Only for both to close in retreat,
Alarmed not because of the virus
But for an act that would fine us.
I raise an elbow, he looks down,
Extending his toe safe in brown.

Digital Messiah

The opportunity was there for you to take:
A desperate world locked indoors, online,
Looking at heaven-blue screens for a sign,
Both Easter and Passover opening the gate –
Yes, you'd have been seen by all at once,
Maybe in a three-piece suit made in Rome,
No, a surgical gown would've best shown
Your concern for the suffering of millions.
The globe waited for your unlined palms
To reconcile not only Christian and Jew,
But Muslim, Hindu, Buddhist, atheist too.
Why didn't you come with outspread arms
When death claimed both hill and crown?
Too late now: the numbers are going down.

Faithful

No, she retorts to her daughter on the phone,
A virus won't keep me from church tonight.
At ten, with candle coloured red and white,
She sets out for an hour's walk on her own.
No-one's outside, doors shut, windows dim,
The Resurrection being live-streamed within.
She waits, like every year, a silent midwife
At the tomb waiting to deliver death to life.
Windows glow, bells open her cryptic heart,
And then the chant: *Hristos anesti ek nekron.*
She does her cross and knocks as though on
The gates of paradise. From the guarded part
A gloved hand extends the candle she yearns,
Whose upright flame she transplants to hers.

---

*   *Hristos anesti ek nekron* – Greek: 'Christ has arisen from the
   dead' – chanted at the Resurrection Service, Easter Saturday
   night.

Anzac

1

This no-man's land between dark and dawn,
With a few isolated clouds, recovering, still,
And sky tinged purple and pinned with stars,
And Southern Cross above the ghostly gum.
Attentive, the neighbours are waiting for six,
Their faces glowing, distant across the street,
More conscious now of their crimson hands
Protecting the candle's bullet-bronze flame.
Having practised the notes the night before,
I finger the silver keys and raise my clarinet –
When a lone magpie takes my breath away,
Warbling, trilling, announcing the advance,
Followed by two kookaburras rattling off
Like Tommy-guns commencing the attack.

2

All those youths in grey are vivid now
That we're retrenched, bunkered down,
Bombarded from blue screen by news
Of casualties growing fast from a few.
The infiltrating enemy has divided us
Not with ribbed grenade but bare hand,
Steeling eyes with fear and mistrust,
Making foe of family, stranger, friend.
At six, though, we'll stand and greet
The Last Post with unguarded breath,
Raising candle and torch to connect
With mates stranded across the street,
Taking heart from youth's sacrifice –
Poppies pinned on chests open to life.

3

Having been in retreat since March,
Time now for the offensive to start:
My raid on the backyard olive tree
Shimmering in its regulation green,
Before the waiting Currawong get
To it with their beaks like bayonets.
Wrestling with each supple branch,
I pick, pluck, strip with bare hands
The rich crop of concentrated light,
When a sniper pricks from the right,
Barely grazing my unprotected eye.
Washing my hands stained black, I
See the blue iris crowned in blood –
My small sacrifice for those I love.

Home Project

Two months of forced isolation at home
And what I've intended for years is done:
I shovelled out the grey top-soil unturned
Since apple orchards coloured the suburb,
Stamped by Wurundjeri soles before that –
Further down I wrestled joyfully for days,
Jackhammering the reef of layered rock,
Raising prized chunks untouched by light
Since the sun started concealing its age –
Formwork removed, steeled concrete set,
I stand in what could be a summer retreat,
Or a cellar for crates of clean-skin wine,
If not a bunker for tomorrow's apocalypse,
A place to sit and read and rest in peace.

Herbal Tea

If I should lose my sense of taste and smell,
And if this disease then infiltrates my lungs
Until the respirator's used on someone else,
(Nature has a way of protecting her young),
My last heaving breath wouldn't be to pray
To some unfigured god who's never known
The curse of ageing, gasping, dying alone,
But to summon that six-year-old from play
And have him follow the cuckoo in spring,
To pluck the stony hill's just-opened eyes
And boil them in a pot that purrs and sings
And fills the evening with contented sighs –
Yes, a breath, my own, it would be enough
To raise me to the tea steaming in his cup.

Football Ground

The oval's spread in last-quarter light:
Four thin shadow are out on their own,
Angled away at forty-five to the spine,
Reaching where an arc should've been,
Giving new meaning, growing length,
To counterparts now cheerless in white.
Still fragrant from this morning's mow,
And with this season's games all away,
Grass is spared boots hunting in packs.
Stilted high between pocket and wing,
The scoreboard's numberless in black,
Visitors screwed tight in namelessness.
In the centre where the circle should be
Two magpies with eyes red from defeat.

Hands

The dominant hand's losing its grip:
In times when work's mainly online
The keyboard's apportioned to both.
They still cooperate, barely touching,
Making music, cooking, tying knots,
And crossing in moments of idleness
Or in mirror image joined in prayer.
But their affair's been more intimate
In this season most virulent with fear:
Washing each other ten times a day,
Slipping and folding left over right,
Scrubbing the other's knuckled back
And arced life-line deeper this year,
Where death's most likely to reside.

Greek Funeral

1

Determined to take her final breath
She slipped past the virus invading
The grilled and gated nursing home –
Ninety-two, she went on her terms,
Leaving strangers masked in white
Stranded in the wake of her pulse.
She'd arranged everything for him:
A plot in a community of Greeks,
The granite's cut, its shade of grey,
The headstone he would engrave,
And depth to be for more than one –
All this she did fierce in her will,
To be the fixed centre of his grief,
A mother bound forever to her son.

2

Mid-winter on the first of May,
Wind-swept rain from the south.
Eight mourners under umbrellas
Shuddering like fruit-bat wings.
A chrome trolley takes the load
Bearers should be shouldering.
The coffin drips on marble steps.
A picnic table's set with tissues
And sanitiser for hands at a loss.
A single candle planted in sand
Won't grow to a glowing crop.
The glassed-in Crucifixion icon
Is crossed with construction tape
Against custom's betraying kiss.

3

It's parked before the alter-screen.
A blonde woman in company blue
And grey gloves turns a silver key
As though opening a dowry chest.
The lid's placed upright on the side,
Where crimson-lipped Judas waits.
Droplets catching candelabra lights
Trickle down to the tessellated floor.
Isolated in black, the chanter starts,
Supported by a downloaded drone.
The priest parts the swinging gates,
Thick-soled runners under his robe.
The old helper extends the censer,
But not kissing the receiving hand.

4

The funeral's more intimate than most,
Despite right hands buried in pockets
Against an urge to reach out and shake,
Or console a shoulder angled in grief.
When the third *Eternal Memory* sounds
With jingling puffs of incensed smoke,
Mourners file past a safe distance apart.
She's on show as on her wedding day,
A touch of blush on her sunken cheeks
And hands folded like a pair of wings.
First to bow and pay his last respects,
He's caught again by those chilling lips
Calling him home from winter's dark –
His only contact with another in weeks.

5

The path dead-ends in a mound of clay,
The horizontal slab has been lifted off,
The coffin lurches lowered in the grave
Filling with water quick from all sides.
Wind snatching his unprotected words
The irate priest abbreviates the hymn,
Sprinkles the prepared wheat and wine,
And shatters bowl and bottle on the lid.
As they all hurry back to waiting cars,
Wiping on grass soles thick with mud,
He looks down into the pooling depth,
Thinking how cruel the weather's been
And Covid for the consolation it denied –
Two weeks later, fifty would've come.

Mathematician

The scientific name had yet to spread
(Nineteen is an unappreciated prime),
Still, he was careful at the conference,
Greeting all from abroad with a nod,
Keeping workshops to fewer than ten –
How did he fall victim to this scourge?
In the weeks of isolation on his back,
Breathless just thinking of his daily run,
He followed induction and fuzzy logic
To that textbook the visitor displayed:
The fractal pattern resembling a crown,
Its glossy cover crackling at his touch.
A die-hard, Neo-Platonist from youth
He'd thought maths impervious to life.

How Many

With words now muffled by face masks,
And those in print pressed like shadows,
Numbers provide the meaning we seek,
The possibility of pattern in randomness,
Sense in the digits proliferating from Pi.
And so we take stock by stopping to ask:
How many positives world-wide today?
(Negatives are safe on zero's other side)
Of these how many were hospitalised,
How many recovered with breath intact?
Of the difference, how many were aged
Less than twenty, more than eighty-five?
And then how many tears to one sorrow,
How many sorrows to a globe in grief?

Dandelion

1

Isolation sharpens our focus on things –
A lone dandelion outgrowing the lawn
Is now more than an unadmired weed:
A glorious giving for all to appreciate,
A crown for the sun losing its strength,
Granny's coin in the march to spring.
When it wilts, fades and turns brown
Its sphere grows gracefully overnight
From a vein-like stem milky with sap,
A gift for the moon in morning light,
A galaxy of seeds connected by hope,
An unearthliness to be wishful again:
A bare breath scatters it far and wide,
Beyond the circumference of its death.

2

Where I'd give it barely a thought,
Now I go down on arthritic knees
To preserve it on a mobile phone:
The future penetrating the present,
Working on sunlight's masterplan
To create a form for its fulfilment:
Beauty, all surface and ephemeral,
Concealing networked scaffolding
Radiating from a desiccated core,
And tempting me with its fragility.
Does beauty also evoke the desire
To destroy the things of delight?
A breath just able to sustain a sigh
Fills space with all that's to come.

Cedar Tree

1

Caught in the pursuit of enriching life,
I've been too time-poor to appreciate
Trees that accompany my being here –
But now that I'm working from home
The time saved on the daily commute
Is spent on the small luxury of gazing
From a window whose varnished slats
Have dulled from angling toward me –
Between meetings accepted on Zoom
And responding to emails flagged red,
I gaze over the screen's isolating hold
At the stillness around passing clouds,
The clearing in the corner of the yard,
Words parting, revealing the cedar tree.

2

Cedrus Deodara, great tree of the gods,
I'm grateful you've reached out to me –
As isolation becomes deeper each day
And mind more estranged from things,
It's easy to imagine only humans exist.
You were the size of a Christmas tree
When the sixties overturned all myths,
Uprooting orchards for housed streets,
Planting you in this quarter-acre plot.
Now, a spatial law in your own might,
You overarch the surrounding fences,
Shadowing the widow's washing line.
You've been approaching since birth,
My arms just able to gather your girth.

3

A Baby Boomer, thought I had it all:
No Great Depression or World Wars,
Mortgage paid off with years to spare,
Aging better than generations before,
Super sufficient to survive me intact –
Ah, but I counted my stars too soon:
The oak's leaves were falling brown
When my own mortality became fact –
The virus had my number in its grip.
My vision suddenly blurred by doubt,
I was saviourless, unanchored, adrift,
When the cedar emerged from the tree,
Rooted deep in its pyramidal height,
Limbs upturned from cradling the sun.

4

Prodigious in giving fully of yourself,
Your generosity has provided purpose
When autumn might've excoriated me –
In the weeks after Easter was annulled,
Before logging-on working from home,
I raked the brown catkins into mounds,
Combing back the lawn needing a cut,
And, with the broom used only for dust,
Swept the yellow pollen scattered fine
Over the veranda, steps, red-brick path,
Imagining it to be the alchemist's gold,
Or granulated light for growing nights,
Or a bare handful of concentrated hope –
The gifted cure for this virus killing us.

5

Spread wide across this suburban space
You catch birds, though seldom to nest,
Holding them by the tips of clawed feet,
And releasing them again to a silent sky
Once they've expressed their innerness,
Which never sounds on extended wings:
Strengthened by your openness to things,
Morning magpies warble the sun awake –
Balanced on your ungovernable height,
War-crying crows claim all they can see –
Answering each other's affectionate call,
Crooning doves caress the afternoon still –
Too small to be seen in shadowed depth,
The finch trills, daring the night to come.

6

After an autumn night constant with rain,
The sun rising in opposition to the moon
Wakes fairy lights from your extremities –
You're both great Christmas tree and gift.
Breathless from shaking and rustling bare
The pin-oaks outgrowing the nature strip,
The wind finds a soulful instrument in you –
Now high with hope, now low and elegiac.
Alpha-male in trunk, your extended limbs
Showcase sister-spider's finest handicraft –
Geometry radiating her livelihood and art.
Today, responding to the lockdown I'm in,
You've created this small opening for me –
More essential than your oxygen I breathe.

7

Keeper of memories and a family's history,
Your shadow discoloured the cubby-house
Once happy as the boxes at Brighton Beach –
My daughters are playing grown-ups inside,
Serving your catkins to their younger selves.
The horizontal limb now touching the fence
Bears the lifelong impression of two rings,
Its growth constricted by the rope tied thick –
They time their swing with nursery rhymes,
Pushing back on gravity with extended legs.
In years to come, what stories will be read
As fingers decipher the annals of your trunk:
The spread of bushfire in the blackest of all?
This isolation in the circle that barely exists?

Dead Gum

Long stripped bare to skeleton
The gum is powerful in death,
More than the humming pylon
Shouldering wired megawatts –
Sunlight fading just after five
Is transformed by ghostly grey
To a glow art can only imagine –
Attracted to its leafless height,
Cockatoos electrify their cries,
Crackling at the solstice night,
Crests incandescent with charge –
After working digitally all day,
I'm regenerated by its surge
Sparking ideas with possibility.

Wattle Tree

1

She lived alone, lights always on,
With her growing family of dolls
Made, painted, ethnically dressed.
A knowing Earth-mother of sorts,
She died at the age of ninety-five,
Just before this pandemic flew in.
Was she also sustenance and sap
To the wattle centred in her yard?
Shortly after her timed departure,
With travel bans locked in place,
Its pale leaves dropped overnight
And it turned black within weeks
Its starkness made more striking
By our olive trees waiting to give.

2

Working from home has benefits,
The small window of opportunity
Between emails received and sent.
For years the solstice would come
And just as unobserved slip away,
Celebrated only by the wattle tree
Blooming in her overgrown yard.
With new restrictions set in place,
I see dearly things no longer there,
Like the midwinter fire we'd light
To keep the growing night in check –
I see again that burst of flowering,
Yellow bright as sulphur or pollen,
Which sustains the hibernating sun.

3

In a few hours the screaming chainsaw
Cleared years of growth from her yard:
Black scarecrow to small, fidgety birds
The bare wattle was dismembered last,
Regurgitated as soaring arcs of mulch.
The grey washing-line appeared intact,
Fully extended, defiant in its triangles,
Three plastic pegs – red, green, brown –
Fixing the winter morning by the seem.
Lockdown opened that moment to me,
And the bird too small to carry a name,
Twitchy on the hoisted pyramid's point,
Trickling silver notes as the coda to this.

Pythagoras' Theorem

If you're unsettled by the nightly news
Of abnormal graphs with deadly spikes,
Here's an exercise to dispel your blues:
From thin air pick a triangle that's right
And draw it with its hypotenuse as base;
Drop the perpendicular from its height,
Forming another two congruent shapes.
(As parentheses in good poetry are tight
This triad's similarity is yours to prove)
Next, letter the lengths, all six in sight,
And make ratios, mind how you choose,
Using the original in pairing like to like.
A dash of algebra and you'll be soothed
By squares offering beauty and delight.

Stillness

1

Busyness can be just as addictive
As speeding on unrestricted roads,
But what of sacrifices in our drive
To reach the oncoming future first?
With mists now descending ahead
I plant the breaks to a jolting stop –
Shaken, thankful, isolated at home.
No more pursuing the imagination
For the prize where parallels meet –
Time now to see things as they are
From a point that's relatively still.
And then, In the space a of breath,
I'm the fixed axle and the wheel,
The end at each instant on the way.

2

Stillness enhanced by thinning fog,
Then the winter sky blank and blue,
And a morning without expectation
Or meaning beyond what simply is.
Bolted to the wall, and shadowless,
A web's strand twitches with shine
In stopping sunlight speeding west.
Breathless from counting its losses,
An oak waits for its last leaf to fall.
The concrete path poured yesterday
Claims the night's light-footed cat.
The back garden eschews all verbs –
Once a swing, the tyre's on its side,
Containing an assortment of herbs.

Bats

Always in black Granny called them *vampiri,*
Warning: be home before the first star appears
Or they'll fill your head, devour your dreams.
A lifetime later, older than she was saying this,
I hear new meaning in that Macedonian word,
Sense the creep of terror in vowels I dismissed.
An evening walk can't dispel the day's unease:
Flocks of silhouettes rise against the sky in ash,
Their flight lugubrious, conjuring a fox's snout,
Furred ears pointed up for navigating the night,
Teeth for nibbling figs, oranges, pomegranates.
Startled by an umbrella opening over my head,
I hurry to the odd-numbered side of the street,
Prodded home by Granny's high-pitched voice.

---

*   *vampiri* – Macedonian: vampires.

Curtain-Raiser

1

A beat of expectation as the sheer curtains part –
Lockdown presenting the commonplace as new:
The winter morning's complete only when seen.
Stripped down to its last denominational leaves
An old pin oak enters the living room shivering.
Approaching clouds crowd the window's space,
Each wanting a name unused to sound its shape.
Caught between sun and star, the ghostly moon
Takes comfort in the circle a coffee cup coined.
Escaping the birthday party forbidden last night,
A tight cluster of red balloons wind-born north
Looms larger than life to walkers gaping below,
Becoming in an instant the crepuscular spheres
Drifting in the background of the evening news.

2

And now, viewers, another pre-breakfast show –
With the sheers too slight for last night's chill,
I draw aside in folds the block-backed drapes,
Revealing a set to make a masked mouth drop:
There, across an unremarkable suburban street,
On the front porch of a neighbour living alone,
A terracotta urn fully eight brick-courses high,
With shadow complementing the wall behind.
Its curvature suggests a pair of uplifting hands,
The creator's mind turning about its fixed will,
An openness to giving shape to water and ash.
Admire its stillness between window and door,
There beneath the brass bell mute for months,
And how we're being gathered in its embrace.

Making

1

The bolt of cotton huffs being unrolled,
Silent when caressed smooth by palms,
The measuring tape's more expressive:
Its numbers rustling, verging on speech.
Cloth mutes the pencil itching to scratch,
But scissors rejoice sounding their part,
Munching crisply across warp and weft,
Crip-crop, crip-crop a hip-hopping beat.
Darting back and forth from sealed lips,
Quick as light, pins keep layers aligned.
The machine grumbles injecting thread,
Pausing to click-clack, setting off again.
There, it's done, a mask for these times –
The price? Hushed words, stifled breath.

2

As a maker and mother in Macedonian*
You've made twenty face-masks today,
Rectangular, the Golden Ratio in each,
Two layers, dense interfacing between,
Made lovingly for relatives and friends
Who'll feel protected leaving the house
And provide assurance to those around.
In the same time what have I produced?
I've also followed a transparent pattern,
Counting syllables for stress and sound,
Layering thought dense with metaphors,
Reflecting your structure in these lines –
Whose meaning an open mouth reveals.

---

* Macedonian: *majka*, pronounced 'maker', means mother.

Decoration

It's been hanging here for months,
Above the stairs' first or last step
(So much in life's a point of view):
This sphere now crimson, not red,
With pimples that spiked overnight.
I wouldn't have given it a thought –
There's nothing so unusual in this,
For things can be both here and not –
But on this mid-autumn afternoon,
With gum-smoke sharpening the air,
I look up from knotting laces tight
To Corona now crowning my head.
When I ask roundaboutly what it is,
My wife rebukes: a Christmas ball.

Incident

He's positioned on the yellow cross,
Waiting to pay for a packet of nails,
Two metres from the youth in front.
Another man appears from the side,
Standing an arm's length from both.
He says nothing, but the youth nods
The intruder to the back of the queue.
'Oh, sorry, mate, I didn't realise you …'
'No worries,' he says, looking down,
Hefting the nails on his cryptic palm.
'Mate, no, you're really crook at me –
That steely look would do Christ in.'
He lowers a mask made of corduroy:
A smile flutters nesting in his beard.

Star

Lockdown, working online deep into dusk,
With this again my only outing for the day:
Twenty-two steps from kitchen to veranda,
And the flap-flap of the checked tablecloth,
Tempting the winter-dark with poppy seed.
The chill's quick to cool my hollow cheeks,
The air's spiced with a neighbour's smoke,
And then, signalling through the cedar tree,
Nameless, numberless, a night-time away,
The star familiar from its splintering wink,
Raising me from growing self-centredness,
Overcoming humankind's grave concerns,
Projecting a life-line from beginning to end:
Seed-virus-I – pinned together by its shine.

Blossom

1

With July spluttering to its primal end
And this winter's isolation still to thaw,
Today I'll defy the law and venture out.
Of all the years chance has allotted me
(Yes, despotic genes are also in the mix)
Sixty-six have passed breath by breath,
The rest will sorely go the way of sighs.
So, I'll drive to the suburb of my youth
And walk the once flower-bedded park
To the plum tree near the footy ground,
To see the first, fearless show of bloom.
Unmasked, drawing deeply on its scent,
I'll summon an adolescent hard at play
And the girls who took his breath away.

2

Racing the clock on my hour's walk,
(My pace is faster than that jogger's
Yet he's exempt from bridled mask)
I see suddenly anew the virgin block
Untouched from when orchards fell,
Rejecting each developer's advance.
In a back corner, as though in retreat,
A neglected peach is blushing pink,
Its branches dark from overnight rain.
Compelled by my heart racing ahead
I high-step through the spikey grass
And, overcoming guilt, snap a sprig –
This isn't young blood running wild,
But a deeper, more considerate love.

3

My younger daughter's in the living room,
Back to the window looking on the street,
Laptop at her fingertips, sipping green tea,
Questioning when this pestilence will end.
I surprise her with my impromptu bouquet.
'Not the heady fragrance of Chanel No. 5,
Nor Bulgari's expensive pentagonal design,
But Nature giving freely her essential best,
This five-fold tribute not only to dark earth
And root but sun and leaf and coming fruit,
Each blossom a censer redolent with hope.'
She appreciates this with a petal-light kiss
And magnifies the sprig in a crystal glass.
I know the old tree has forgiven my crime.

Work Wear

Unbodied for months, long-sleeved shirts
Hang in resignation from question marks.
Trousers, pressed with unwanted creases,
Pockets upside down and empty of want.
Laces lessened by a double-knotted bow,
Shoes softly in-soled for darkness to nest.
With mirrors ignored, beards flourishing,
The razor has turned on the bristly brush.
Glasses that brought the distant sign near
Gaze cross-armed, blurring my fingertips.
Untouched in days, black fading to grey,
The wallet bulging with numbered cards.
Behind the laptop, its silver band spread,
The watch, cold, untimed from my pulse.

Religion

1

If the way we work is changing by the week,
And greetings like kissing the other's cheek,
Will religions founded traditionally on stone
Survive faith being practiced online, alone?
Are we less good or more susceptible to sin
Now that the exemplary text isn't echoed in
Rowed church, mosque, temple, synagogue?
Are we more distant from our choice of God
Having crossed months without communion,
Without loud declarations chanted in unison,
Without clerics and their intermediary roles,
And bowing to the stranger's upturned soles?
Will the times enshrine our heart with grace,
Restoring God to His, Hers, Its rightful place?

2

They're not immune to what's in the air:
Pan, whose glance scattered partridges,
Fell to an arrow overshooting the mark.
The pantheon would follow in his wake
As much from lightning revealing itself
As the smell of herbed lamb on the spit.
Will the one I've plucked from nowhere
And coloured with imagination at night
Survive this pandemic now shaping me?
With unseen digits proliferating virally,
Has heaven been uploaded to the cloud,
To be accessed by password not prayer?
Will my god emerge stronger from this,
Like Yahweh from the Shoah's smoke?

3

'Unprecedented', yes, but only in our lives –
(The media can't see past the here and now)
The Black Plague was worse on every count,
Spread by fleas piggy-backing a host of rats
Flitting at night like today's suspected bats.
But new ways of knowing and making arose
From what must've seemed the apocalypse.
The angled glow of the Renaissance shone
On Tuscany's shadowed windows and walls.
The Reformation's god was accessible to all,
And Science overcame fear of the unknown.
What awaits us when we've tallied our dead
And stored the breathless respirators away?
The place where humanity will finally arise?

4

God's form changes after each plague:
Turning his back on locusts and frogs
And hybrid deities crowding his mind,
Moses endured sand stinging his eyes
To breathe four consonants with faith,
Each like grit at the back of his throat.
When the Black Death went as it came,
The age needed a contemporary look:
The Pantocrator in Byzantium's dome
Became Rome's strong-armed Creator,
His nose more Florentine than Jewish.
For us, when the pandemic has passed,
God might shed both image and name,
Becoming our encrypted code instead.

Spring Cleaning

Confined to homes by lockdown and curfew,
We look for liberation in whatever's at hand:
In shelved basement, garage, backyard shed
We consider the store of 'it might be of use',
With each thing occasioning that tug-of-war
Between memory and a possibility of space,
Between being and a fear of being undefined.
Still, we feel lighter when the future prevails
And we discard the slatted cot laced in webs,
The set of three suitcases all packed into one,
Fittings and fixtures fashion turned into junk,
Cans of paint whose lids rust has sealed tight –
On the nature strip, the plum tree in blossom
Blesses the trash with a sprinkling of white.

Encounter
(With a nod to Ogden Nash)

Today, on my permitted hour of exercise,
Walking past the back of Odyssey House,
Which was once a Franciscan monastery,
I was surprised not by the local kangaroo
But three furry, long-necked quadrupeds
Indigenous to a continent cooler than this.
With life becoming less visionary by day,
This was a presentation mythical in scope.
The first nodded and, through half a smile,
Said he's often taken for a Tibetan priest.
The second fixed me with its slitted eyes
And claimed to hail from Peru's Willama.
The third, in tones darkly lateral, elegiac,
Sang of old Lllama, an Albanian ancestor.

Online Funeral
(Pandelis E. 19.8.2020)

1

Left-clicking the blue underlined link,
I'm both a prisoner in my living room
And participant in their hour of grief,
Along with the camera always unseen.
Ten mourners, seated alone or paired,
Gaze at the coffin angled to the right,
Lid closed to keep all memories intact,
My imagination open entirely to him.
No hymns, here, no incense, no icons,
Nothing to lessen death's giving back:
From scripted eulogies, broken words,
The warmth of one's unmasked breath,
Each of us composes the man he was,
Composing myself for what's to come.

2

He steps lightly from his family's sighs,
And, defying restrictions on going out,
Delivers me to a distant time and place –
And there he stands, tall as a poplar tree,
Cheekbones blazing like pomegranates,
His hands shaped by mountain and lake:
The groom, carnation bright in his lapel,
Tragic in *Macedonian Blood Wedding*,*
Weaving hemp with hope by candlelight,
Crucified to stone on barren Makronisos**
From which he arises in evangelic faith,
Offering a village boy the coveted apple
When others would've driven him away –
He has given me that very apple in this.

---

*   *Macedonian Blood Wedding* – a drama by Vojdan
    Chernodrinski.

** Makronisos – island near Athens used as a prison during the
    Greek Civil War 1946–49.

Two Kookaburras

High up on power lines humming their electric blues
A pair of kookaburras (seldom seen other than in twos)
Erupts in a sound going back to when time was young:
Together at first, staccato, indistinguishable from one,
Then breaking off, alternating in solo interlude as each
Tries to outdo the other in how far their voices reach,
Until their cacophony subsides in catching their breath,
When, heads raised, they explode in a concluding duet,
Koo-koo-ka-ka-koo-koo-koo-koo-ka-ka-koo-koo-ka-ka,
Stopping me near the Yarra's rush in Westerfolds Park.
Such unrestrained joy in what's been months of gloom:
Are they celebrating the wattle just beginning to bloom,
Or mocking a masked walker unable to smile and say
So much as a clear hello to those walking the other way?

On Turning Seventy
(For Michael P.)

Defying this divisive plague,
Here you stand, dear friend,
Wholly three score and ten,
Bearded like a biblical sage.
There'll be no celebration,
No handshake, forget a kiss –
But you're accepting of this:
The law's your consolation.
The decade will turn and pass
Faster than the one before,
When, at your fourth score,
We'll gather to raise a glass
Of clear home-brewed *rakija,*[*]
Wishing you a hundred years.

---

[*] *rakija* – Macedonian: a strong whisky.

Spring

With Stage Four restrictions pushing into spring
Are we kept in line by threat of fines that sting,
Or a sense of civic duty accompanied by guilt?
Either way, it seems the season's impulsive lift,
That buoyancy of youth, is now easily subdued.
We're free, you say, to choose not only the cut
But the pattern imprinted on the cloth for masks.
Yes, this mitigates the severity of surgical white
But what of muffled speech and thwarted breath?
In Bulleen's Birrurung Park, as people walk left
On the circular path, Nature goes the other way:
Wattle breaking winter's grip with flagrant gold,
Unruly gang-gangs protesting with crests ablaze,
Covid signs stripped away by last night's storm.

Junk

With the curfew undefining the weeks
I'm more attentive walking the streets,
Starting from the centredness of home,
To the circumference of restricted zone.
With curiosity unleashed, ahead of me,
It rummages freely for image or simile
Among the junk waiting on nature strip
For keen recyclers or cartage to the tip.
With folk preparing for refurbishments
I'm renewed by things chance presents:
A child's three-wheeler, speckled silver,
Riding on the back of a vacuum cleaner,
Old shoes in a car tyre bald as bitumen,
Two fish tanks, an oven gaping at them.

Wind

The forecast is for fierce wind this afternoon –
Working online, at home, facing the window,
I'm surprised by sunlight glancing off leaves,
The shadow of white sheets fixed to the wall.
By noon stirring air has stiffened to a breeze
Frisking the bare pin oak in front of the house,
Deflowering the magnolia's penitential cups,
Gathering recalcitrant clouds to a single flock.
At four it has strengthened to full-blown wind
Wrestling for sole possession of the cedar tree,
Littering the suburb with cockatoos and crows.
It's five and the washing's beating in surrender –
But encouraged by the hour's unrestricted howl,
I throw all caution to the open-mouthed vowel.

Black Achan Pear Tree
(Ruffey Lake Park, Templestowe)

1

Last of the orchard that lined these slopes
Which early settlers cleared of defiant gums,
The old pear tree's still holding its ground
A child's wish from swings bound in tape.
Bedraggled in autumn and in winter bereft,
It's caught in the squeeze of hardening sap –
A scarecrow to cockatoos unseen in months.
This starkness catches my divided attention
As I catch my breath thwarted by this mask,
And I see again last summer's full offering
Hanging like bells replete, ripe with sound.
I interrupt my timed walk to caress its bark,
As if a grandparent's hand stroked in thanks,
Mindful of the darkness hollowing its trunk.

2

Early September, the curfew still in force
And set to remain until this second wave
Washes over and ebbs horizontally away,
Claiming livelihoods along with the dead.
Shouldering the wisdom of greying years,
I'm suspicious of saviours in black masks
(Charming as some undertaker's assistant)
Promising a way to the curve's flattening.
It has become my sustenance and strength,
The reason I'm out on a sanctioned walk,
Past varieties of trees already in blossom,
Down to the creek that's outrun its course,
Looking for a red bud, a pimple on a twig,
Hope in this season of disease and despair.

3

On this the fifteenth holy day of spring,
It's time we stopped lamenting our loss
And walked between crescent and cross
To what sun and earth commune to bring.
And so let's toss aside the sterile masks
To breathe deep of this late blossoming,
Fill mouths with renewed light and sing
In praise of this unappreciated patriarch.
Let's take each other's unwashed hands
To make a strong but lively human ring,
Blow all our fears to the wind and dance
Around this much-hoped-for awakening –
A few white petals opening in defiance
Of drying sap and life's slow hollowing.

4

The thirteenth day of a quiet Christmas
(Not a drum for yesterday's Epiphany),
Unmasked faces glow striding the park
Spread with summer like buttered bread.
Hallowed be the darkness in your trunk
For today's overflow of leaves and fruit –
This undeserved gift to be savoured last,
For which isolation has served me well,
As fasting purified my earthy ancestors.
I approach you as though a sacred site
And reach for the pear intended for me,
Hanging still, heavy as the human heart.
As I partake of your sweet selflessness,
You find fulfilment by becoming flesh.

Maternal Advice

Yes, my girl, I've heard your complaint:
That sterile mask does nothing for you –
Mine is silk-layered with a poppy print.
Please, wear it safely leaving the house,
As grandma wore her *niqab** at your age.
And be sure to cover your glowing face
Not just against a temptation to be vain
(Beauty showing off for immodest gain
Is sinful, to be avoided like this plague)
But to keep the invader from your lips,
Who comes red-crowned from the East
Singing there's no danger to the young.
Yes, you'd be another breathless bride
In that haram veiled in perpetual shade.

---

*   *niqab* – veil worn by some Muslim women to cover the hair,
     nose and mouth.

Zero

1

Numbers must fall from breathless highs,
The second wave shamble along the shore,
For restrictions to be lifted from our lives –
Forget wage rise, profit, budget surpluses,
Zero's become the new meaning of more,
A silver bullet against infinitesimal mites,
The Holy Grail producing much from less,
If nothing else the table-cloth's ring-stain
From the last supper nobody got to enjoy.
Zero, grasped wholly in the dead of night
With both pupils open wide to possibility:
The halo covering the many-spiked crown,
The no thing existing fully in its paradox,
The divisor that takes us to the other side.

2

Today's announcement of no new cases
Is celebrated by elbows angled at acute,
Mouths gaping at the successful pursuit
Behind masks so much part of our faces
We forget them raising our glass of red.
Zero, our halo for months of lockdown,
The eradication of the mutating crown
Whose impression has marked our heads,
The opening we've all been waiting for,
And through which each of us must pass
To enjoy what the future guards in store –
A world safe, gloriously normal at last.
And yet has that state ever been attained?
For the living normal is constant change.

Eyes And The Mask

Passing a walker going the other way
At a speed twice that of my approach,
I'd see their eyes as part of the whole,
Alert more to the shape of their nose:
Was it small, snubbed, long, aquiline?
And then the lips: were they pressed
In conceit or about to loosen a smile?
Followed by the complementing chin:
Was it raised, taunting fate to punch,
Or low, demure, avoiding the crowd?
With the mask covering half the face,
The eyes are now centre of attention:
Does her glare and look-away reflect
A stare unbecoming of an older man?

My Father's X-Rays

1

Cleaning out the damaged filing cabinet
Burglars jemmied open twenty years ago,
I'm stopped by a large, yellow envelope
Under books for grandchildren to come:
Rows of dated stickers, a patient number,
My father's name and birthdate in bold
From when another burglar came unseen,
Coursing arteries narrowing to his heart,
And from there breaking into his brain,
Ransacking its order, stealing memories,
Leaving him nothing but an empty look.
It's early spring, the day's overcast, still –
I press the envelope to my ribbed chest,
Thinking: sun's needed for what's inside.

2

A few days later, it's the spring equinox,
Light and dark balanced on an olive leaf,
Crows and cockatoos in competing cries,
A white mask left breathless on bitumen.
Outdoors, I raise high the quivering film,
Startled by images stark in natural light:
Ribs that curved around hope and desire,
Cavity where the triple bypass was done,
The heart contracted to a fistful of shade,
The wide pelvic plate, hip joints arthritic,
Cartlidge thinned in fields and factories,
And lower, almost embarrassed to look,
The nothing from which I was conceived,
Now eclipsing in a blur the morning sun.

3

A series of timed shots taken from above
That resemble the cauliflower's negative,
Or the kernel of a walnut cleanly cracked –
Can words traverse this twisting labyrinth
To find the man who didn't say good-bye?
Are you present in that inky spot recalling
Your thumbnail black from a painful hit?
Is the cloudy patch in the left hemisphere
Grief for your dear wife's untimely death?
And is that grey swirl above the right ear
The enduring echo of monotonous waves
That brought you here in a borrowed case?
Or are you in that pupil between sockets,
Watching, holding my image in the film?

Supermarket

Is that Margaret at the discounted bread?
If only the mask covered less of her face.
And if she weren't wearing white gloves
I'd know at once from her diamond rings.
But Margaret's hair's always dyed dark,
Not in need of a cut, roots showing grey.
And she's in runners, loose trackie daks,
Not the usual heels and designer slacks.
Should I approach her, say a quick hello,
Apologise if a stranger's voice replies?
Oh, she's looked at me and turned away.
'Hi, Margaret, have you been to the gym?'
No, she can't turn up her new nose now,
And put me down with that Botox smile.

Snail Watching

There's time now for slower things:
I observe a snail's punctuated flow,
Smoothing the present as it moves,
Leaving a trail of silver in the past –
Pimple-ended probes are swaying,
Glistening, extended to full length,
Quick to retract at something felt,
Its body frothing safely in its shell.
Have our eyes evolved from these?
Flesh reaching for the airy future,
Becoming finer than a ray of light,
Touch transformed to distant sight –
As clouds approach, I hurry inside,
Footprints left behind on the grass.

Platypus

In the Yarra vigorous after spring rain
A platypus is putting on a lively show
(Who knows, perhaps more than one)
For watchers on the suspended bridge:
Surfacing here and there like a carp,
Floating, head almost identical to tail,
As it takes a breath, then duck-dives,
Disappearing, keeping all in suspense,
Before slipping out there in surprise.
Wonder best expressed when shared,
The audience forget social distancing
And lower masks better to be heard.
'It's neither this nor that,' a man says.
A child asks, 'What's a platypus for?'

Kangaroo

Unlike before, lockdown sees crowds
Flocking happily to Westerfolds Park:
Walkers breathing hot in their masks,
Open-mouthed cyclists turning uphill,
Parents and children still not at school.
This increased presence and curiosity
Has made the kangaroos more at ease,
Whether on their flanks in open grass
Or upright, small heads facing the sun.
Today, instead of lookout for the mob,
A grey rose to the fullness of its height
As a young woman crept closer to him –
Poised, powerful, in a cinematic pose,
Springing after her smartphone clicked.

Two Masks

Their masks left out on the washing line,
Aflutter in the breeze warming to spring,
Hers blue, with poppies like open mouths,
His wholly black, cut from coarser cloth.
They haven't seen eye to eye in a decade,
Back when children were their only focus,
As each waited for the other first to speak
Silence hardened and widened their divide.
They sit on the veranda, he sipping coffee
And scrolling an iPad for the day's graphs,
She jasmine tea, knitting an infant's wrap,
Both isolated as weathered garden gnomes.
Lightened of breath's heaviness in pleats,
Two masks are playing kiss me if you can.

Games

Playing Cops and Robbers in our lane,
I'd use Dad's hankies ironed in fourths –
Mum's, pink and too small for my need.
I'd unfold it square on a bluestone step,
Halve it by re-folding along a diagonal,
And then cover my face with a triangle,
Tying it at the back with a double knot.
We'd swap when Robbers were caught.
In this grown-up version now the rage,
The goodies hide behind a telling mask,
Baddies fined for thumbing their noses.
Today, observing distance at the ATM,
I was stopped, disconcerted, surprised –
A masked stranger had stolen my eyes.

Old Greek

He could've been walking the Agora
When plague darkened the Parthenon,
But Socrates was in Oakleigh instead,
Addressing himself through his mask:
If life's worth is measured by its end,
I've planned it all, paying in advance:
The coffin mahogany, silver trimmed,
Two priests with chanters either side,
A headstone to dazzle mourning eyes,
A three-course lunch and toast to me.
Ah, but the virus has plans of its own:
If it decides to follow me home today,
And at this age the chances are high,
No more than ten people could attend.

Brick Paving

Freedom confined to the backyard,
My thoughts two white butterflies
Flitting at will from thing to thing,
As I pave where grass won't grow
Angled down on hands and knees.
Let's say the red brick's a syllable,
I lay ten across for the line I need,
This rubber mallet thudding each,
Ensuring right's parallel to the left,
And the spacing's uniformly wide.
The eleventh row, a rhythm found,
Pattern emerges of its own accord,
And then, without reason or rhyme,
It comes together in fourteen lines.

Iron Mask

Restrictions allowing gatherings of five,
Though still up to five kilometres away,
We drive out to Bulleen's Banksia Park,
Our masks lowered for coffee and cake.
Having not been fed in several months,
Magpies swoop down on sharper wings.
On the grassy slope above where we sit,
And positioned for passing traffic to see,
A rectangle stands slouched to the right,
Shining like a blacksmith's sooted brow,
With an narrow slit for viewing the past
And beyond to what the future conceals.
'Ned Kelly's helmet,' our daughter says.
'People have lost their daring these days'.

Three Coffees

Three men, each with different coloured mask,
The sum of their ages more than they'll admit,
Are waiting as one for ordered coffee to arrive.
'When my time comes,' says the one in brown,
'I've made it clear: bury me in Fawkner's clay,
Surrounded by sky, crosses, and names I know.'
Lively eyes bloodshot, the one in crimson says,
'I want to go out dancing in flame's embrace,
My ashes to be scattered as the clarinet plays.'
The third, in blue, turns from the raucous creek:
'I've willed to be weighted feet-first in the sea,
To join my granddad who didn't make it here'.
They remove their masks and sip through froth,
The coffee heavenly despite polystyrene cups.

Perfume Maker

This is no time for demure scents,
They must be bolder to infiltrate
The mask that has emptied shops –
Burnt sandalwood, amber, musk,
Dried cedar and Samarkand rose,
Evoking that first kiss in the park,
Winter opening its fist to spring,
The moment twilight turns to ash.
What is the purpose of perfume?
Is the touch on her sinewed neck
Meant to enhance her self-esteem
Or surprise another with delight?
Or, like the cut and colour of hair,
Both a public and private affair?

Love and Corona

Restaurants, cafes, cinemas closed,
Homes at least five kilometres apart,
They texted, Zoomed, met in parks,
Well-groomed for the hour's walk.
Winter gathered its flocks of crows,
But their fire was gaining strength,
Stoked by each mask-muffled word,
Prohibited breath, sanitised caress,
And wind prowling deserted streets.
Young and fit, no symptoms of flu,
They bridled desire with civic sense
And arranged to undertake the test –
Never was the product of negatives
Celebrated with such a positive kiss.

Heraclitus*

He's often called The Obscure,
This for his cryptic apothegms
Which were intended as a cure
For cases of fixed mindedness.
I've never dipped my bare toes
In the same brown Yarra twice,
And despite the westward flow
My image is still on the surface.
Each low step on Escher's stairs
Leads at once both to the tower
And the dungeon's stinking air.
He was so prescient seeing our
Times: life in the other's death
And dying in a stranger's breath.

---

*   Heraclitus – pre-Socratic Greek Philosopher. M.C. Escher –
      Dutch graphic artist whose work is inspired by geometry.

Dead Gum Tree at Sunset

As an exercise in suspending disbelief
Turn away a moment from reading this
To imagine a painting of Templestowe:
A clearing back-dropped by bluish hills,
Green-grey bush and shrub pulling back
From the gum centred imposingly dead,
Verging bone-white from wind and rain,
With cockatoos boisterous on its crown,
Their sulphur crests proliferating moons,
Evening gold barely touching the trunk
Reflected in the pool doubling its height.
On this side of a rusty barbed-wire fence
A man, masked in blue, and almost old,
Standing in its shadow slender and long.

Crow

The scene is composed by creative chance:
Last light lengthening shadows tissue-thin
Across Bonds Road ending in Yarra scrub
And grass bowed by the weight of its seed,
A horse grazes this side of Odyssey House,
Its shit enriching the breeze otherwise bare.
A man directs his camera's cyclopean stare
At a crow clawed to a post weathered grey,
Its polished beak pointing at the crusty sun,
Wings heavy from flight, eyes yellow, still.
The white mask fluttering around my wrist,
I stand behind him, restraining each breath –
Clicking, he catches my shadow next to his,
Along with the crow now flying low, west.

S/He

Weeks of isolation hardened their silence,
Which began before corona chilled the air
Over criticism he'd been unable to accept.
Sitting uncoupled, well apart at breakfast,
She tap-tap-taps with the back of a spoon,
Each strike crunchier than the one before,
Rolling loose the cooling shell on the sink
And then peeling it off like wrinkled skin –
With this his ego also suddenly gives way
To that softer self arrogance has protected.
He feels again her alert, rounded fingertips
Holding him in that moment of tenderness,
Her lips opening as though to take him in,
Teeth biting into his flesh running like yolk.

Natural Fear

1

Lockdown crowding Westerfolds Park
From breakfast through to dinner time,
Today I go out for my exercise at dusk,
Crossing the narrow suspension bridge
As the Yarra follows traces of the sun,
Past Odyssey House, dome withdrawn
Against a clear sky deepening in blue.
Each step sharpens the crescent moon,
Different greens turn to common grey,
The asphalt path curves toward a hill.
From what appear shrubs just in sight
Kangaroos arise, alert to my approach –
Alone, surrounded by nature and night,
I turn and run, not daring to look back.

2

The return's overlooked going forward –
I'm trailing my heart now racing ahead.
Stars are scratching through in the east,
The moon's more pointed at both ends,
Long, low hoots sound between breaths,
Ghostly limbs reach out from the sides,
Hissing grass raises the hair on my neck.
A Wurundjeri presence springs to mind
And suddenly I'm guilty of trespassing,
Violating their place by just being here.
I hurry, over the boardwalk and bridge,
Through the carpark empty at this hour
To light spilling on the dead-end street –
Grateful for the safety arising from fear.

Vale
(Peter G.)

You were a man of steel throughout your life,
Steadfast in the practice of custom and belief,
Yet melting in compassion for those in strife
With a generosity born of your adopted name.
'God calls me,' you'd reply, when asked why.
'I'm the rivet needed for creation to progress.'
Go lightly, dear *braté,* to that clearing ahead,
Accompanied by drum and the clarinet's high
Sounding the *pushteno* for your spirit to soar.
Lead us to those picnics near Mount Macedon,
And beyond, to the house you built in *Banitsa*,
Where now you stand in welcome at the door,
Extending *dobro doidi* to stranger and friend,
With wine, wheat, *rakija* and imprinted bread.

---

*   Macedonian: *braté* – bother, *pushteno* – a lively dance, *Banitsa*
     – former name of the village of Vevi, *dobro doidi* – welcome,
     rakija – strong whisky

Kookaburra

Kookaburras laugh fullest in pairs –
Alone, this didn't stutter a syllable
Perched on the cedar's lower limb
Rope-ringed where our girls' swing
Swept them to joy's loudest height.
How pensive, sombre, it appeared,
Looking down at our patchy lawn,
Staring beyond its horizontal beak
Toward the echoings of yesterday,
Withdrawn, wrapped still in wings,
Waiting like an owl for the night.
We watched from our garden seat,
Empty nesters, each seeing ahead,
Together in love's silence and loss.

Spiral

Beginning from a nothinged point,
The unwinding of a galaxy grows,
Becoming lawn seed swept in arcs
Against a sky ploughed by thunder,
Becoming a heart-sized pine cone
On which hope finds its way back,
Becoming the curve of silver trails
Left spotted on concrete by snails
Now curled in shells like embryos,
Becoming the course of this virus
Long exponentially out of control,
Becoming the whorls of fingertips
Imprinted on a clear oxygen mask,
Breath swirling, condensing, cold.

Being Open

Isolation fosters an openness to things:
The butcherbird's twa twi-twi-twi twa
Brings to mind this suburban evening,
Speaks to me of autumn's falling stars.
And the creek straggling around rocks,
Thinning, pausing a moment in a pool,
Draws me to the distant bay it yearns.
Musing at the window this afternoon,
I was both the observer and observed,
Passing moment and ornamental clock:
Rising above the season's constraints,
Moving to an end merging with mine,
Clouds, not as drought-breaking rains,
Performing a breathtaking pantomime.

A Lesson

With schools closed another week
The boy, no more than five or six,
Slips from his grandfather's grip
And walks backwards facing him,
Counting aloud from ten to zero.
'Grandpa' he says, staying in step,
'Why do you use a walking stick?'
'To prod this path when it slows
'And move it forward just for us,
'Otherwise it would stop at once
'And hurry back to where it starts,
'Leaving only emptiness in front.'
'Grandpa, don't prod it anymore –
'I'm tired and my feet are so sore.'

Celebrations

Today delivers a double celebration:
A year since fear masked our mouths
And hope lay in unseen calculations,
The vaccine arrives to sighs out loud,
Though still to be kept potently inert
Until roused by the warmth of blood
To uncrown this virus threatening us,
Securing again our primacy on earth.
Having divided the darkness by time,
Perseverance landing softly on Mars
Is greeted by hands clapping all fives –
Its mission, to uncover buried avatars
And water for tomorrow's outer post,
For us to humanise our universal host.

Full Moon Rising

With the virus now baring arms in flight
And restrictions eased on wearing masks,
I breathe aloud walking just before dark,
Set on the view from Westerfolds' height.
Standing looking east, sky finely veiled,
I'm soon joined by a knowing kangaroo
That squats upright on bent legs and tail,
Its small paws folded in devoted attitude.
Then, from the fringe of silhouetted trees,
A tinge, a glow, a show of annunciation:
The moon rising, whole, ochre crowned,
Heavy on the horizon in borrowed gown,
Gathering me come from afar, as it's done
To generations of wide-eyed Wurundjeri.

Catching The Light

The last day of a summer barely seen:
(Still, it's better we burned with fever,
Endured oxygen sighing condolences,
Than last February's suffocating fires.)
Filtering through the city-settled haze,
Evening light gives meaning to stone,
It brushes the pin oak's vibrant leaves
With only the presentiment of yellow,
Returning to the rose singular in white
Its image charcoaled live on concrete.
Corona has marked not only our flesh,
Stamping us with the signature of Cain,
But the sun, now setting red as it goes,
Staining a spread of cloud fine as gauze.

Grazing

Autumn evening, just north of the Yarra,
Sunlight breaches a bank of low clouds,
Skims this rural valley in the city's grip.
On the wide flat electric wire has fenced
Cattle are grazing shadow-covered grass,
Heavy-headed, bellied with gravity's fill,
Hooves becoming more rooted each day.
On the river side of the homestead's hill
Kangaroos congregate in a patch of glow,
Faithful, small heads raised, gazing west,
The slipping light catching on their paws,
Their senses long-attuned to air not earth
Now open, taking in this uplifting grace
For tomorrow's spring to verge on flight.

Training Night

Having been sidelined more than a year
(Covid's still distant as old age to them)
Forty hopefuls are sweating to impress
For the season opener just two days off.
The oval is greener than it's ever been,
Its purpose restored by circle, arc, line,
While whiter against the crowding dark
Lustrous goalposts wait in tight corsets.
Boys cocooned in lockdown and curfew
Are now youths centred in their shadows
Like stamen with its petals drawn aside,
Their voices breaking in the cooling air,
Their faces crimson, bursting with breath,
Set on stardom forged by towering lights.

Red Moon
(26.5.2021)

The night sky has cleared for the show,
More stars than expected have appeared,
Fidgeting like children forced to be still.
We gasp as one at the prefigured glow
From behind a neighbour's angled roof,
And take turns scanning with monocular
Until the moon fully occupies our sight:
Sharp in silver, having shed her weight,
Edging by slivered arcs to total eclipse,
Crowned red for what tomorrow brings.
A magpie warbles now suddenly alone,
Two dogs howl from the dead-end street,
My wife's misty words catch on a sigh,
Her grip tightening on my cooling wrist.

Printed in Australia
Ingram Content Group Australia Pty Ltd
AUHW022332250424
393529AU00003B/12